For curious minds and bright hearts, this book was created with the incredible help of artificial intelligence, a magical tool that, like you, is always eager to learn and discover new things.

S.S

2024

This Book Belongs to:

◆———————————————————————◆

Test Color Page

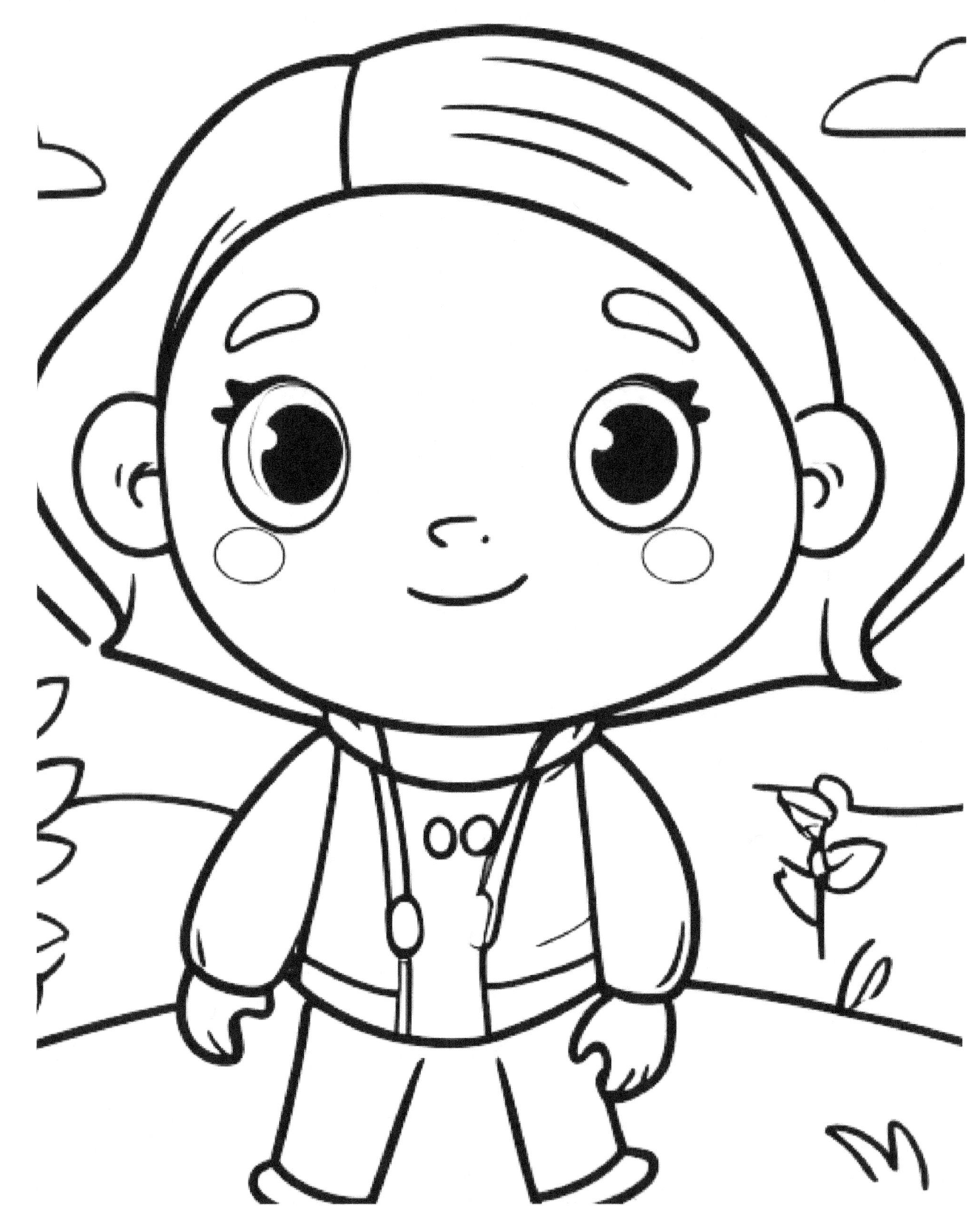

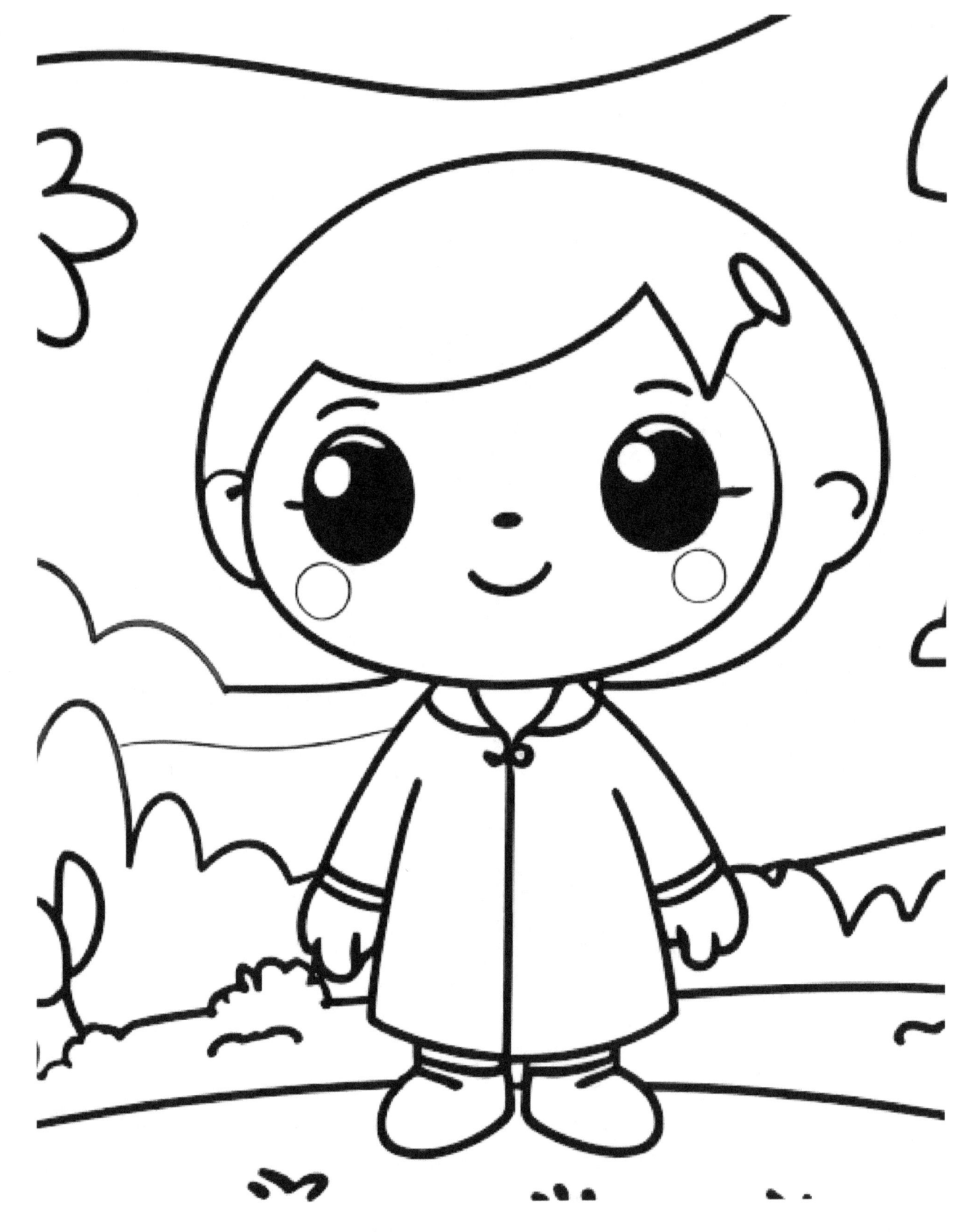

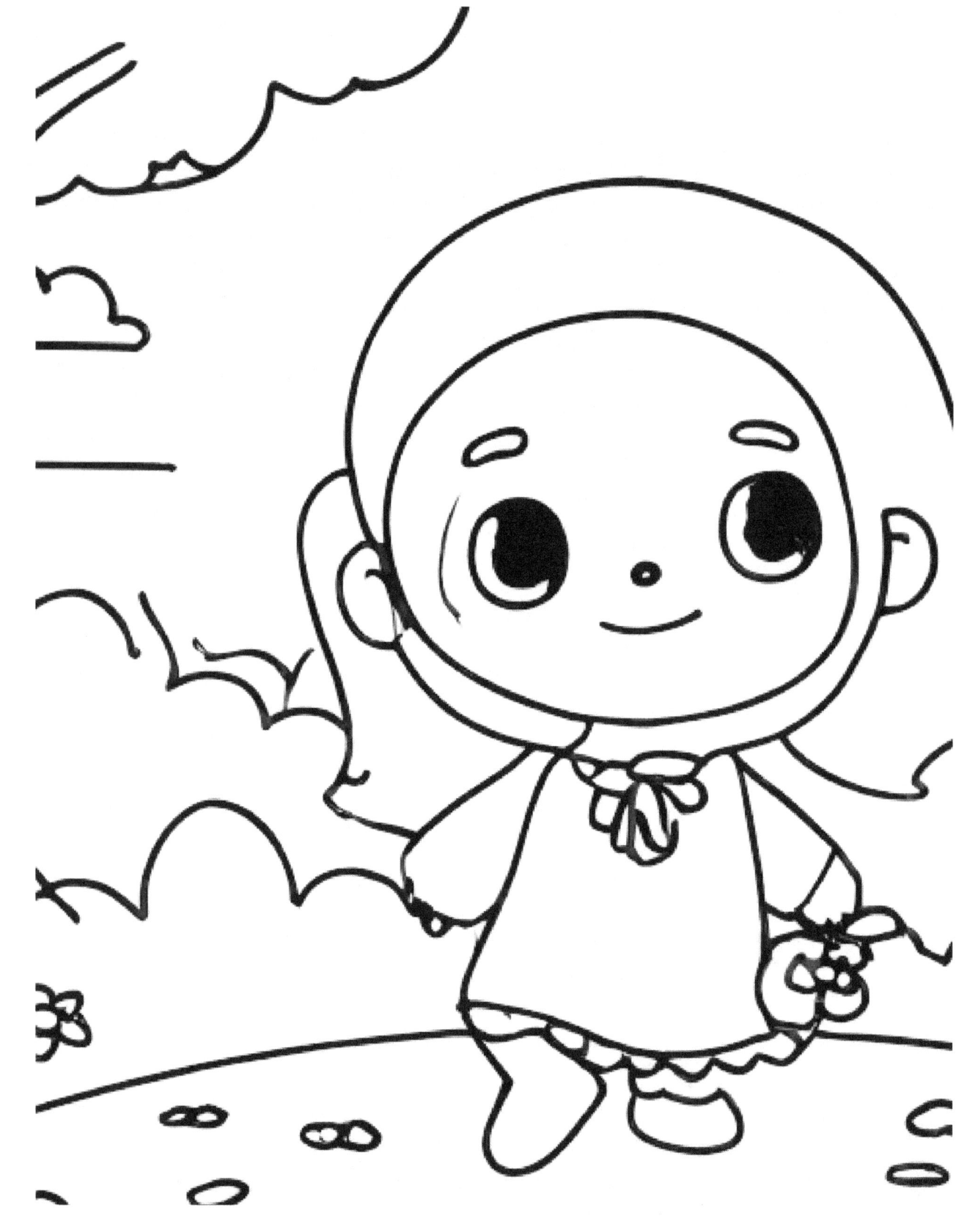

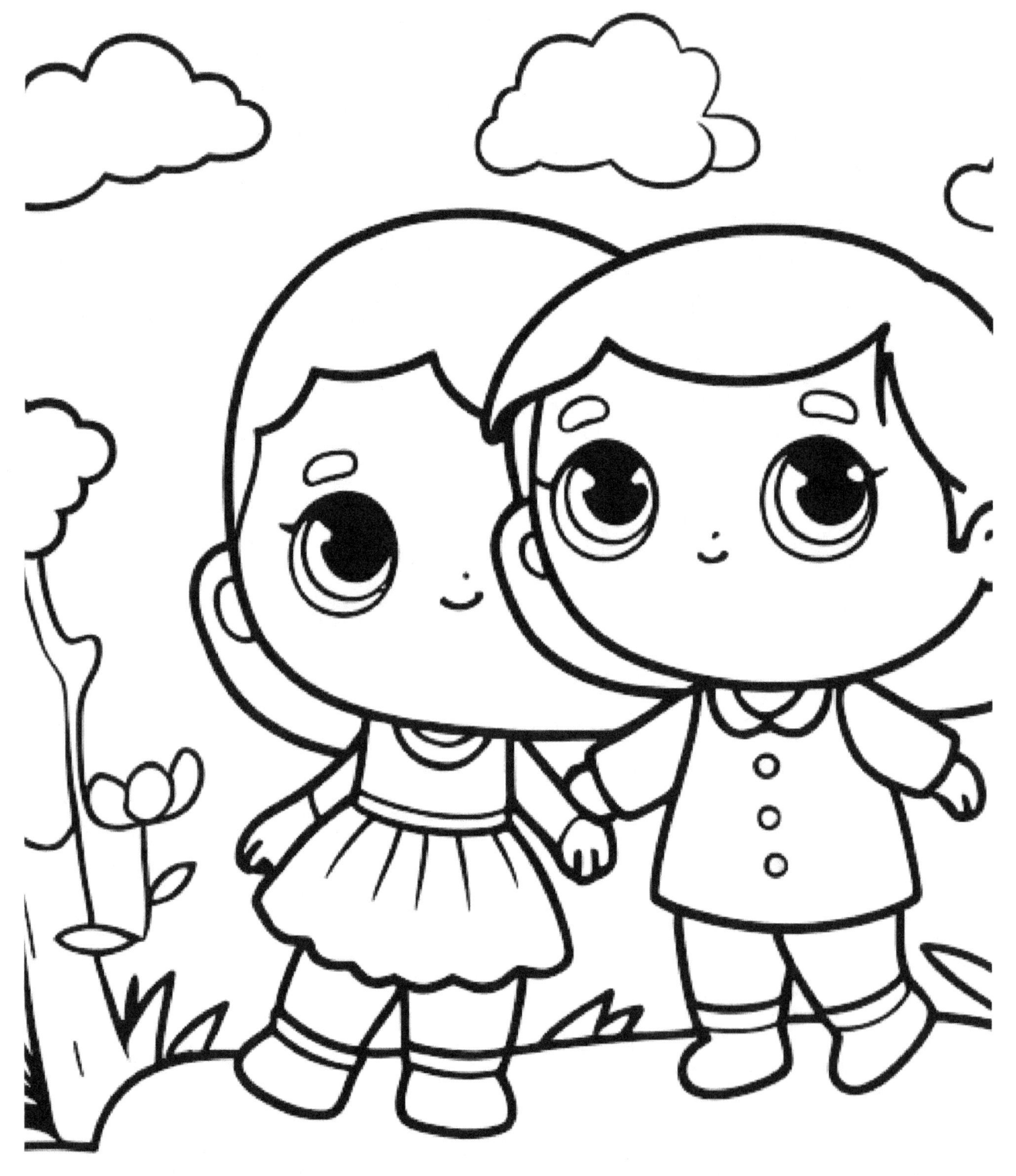

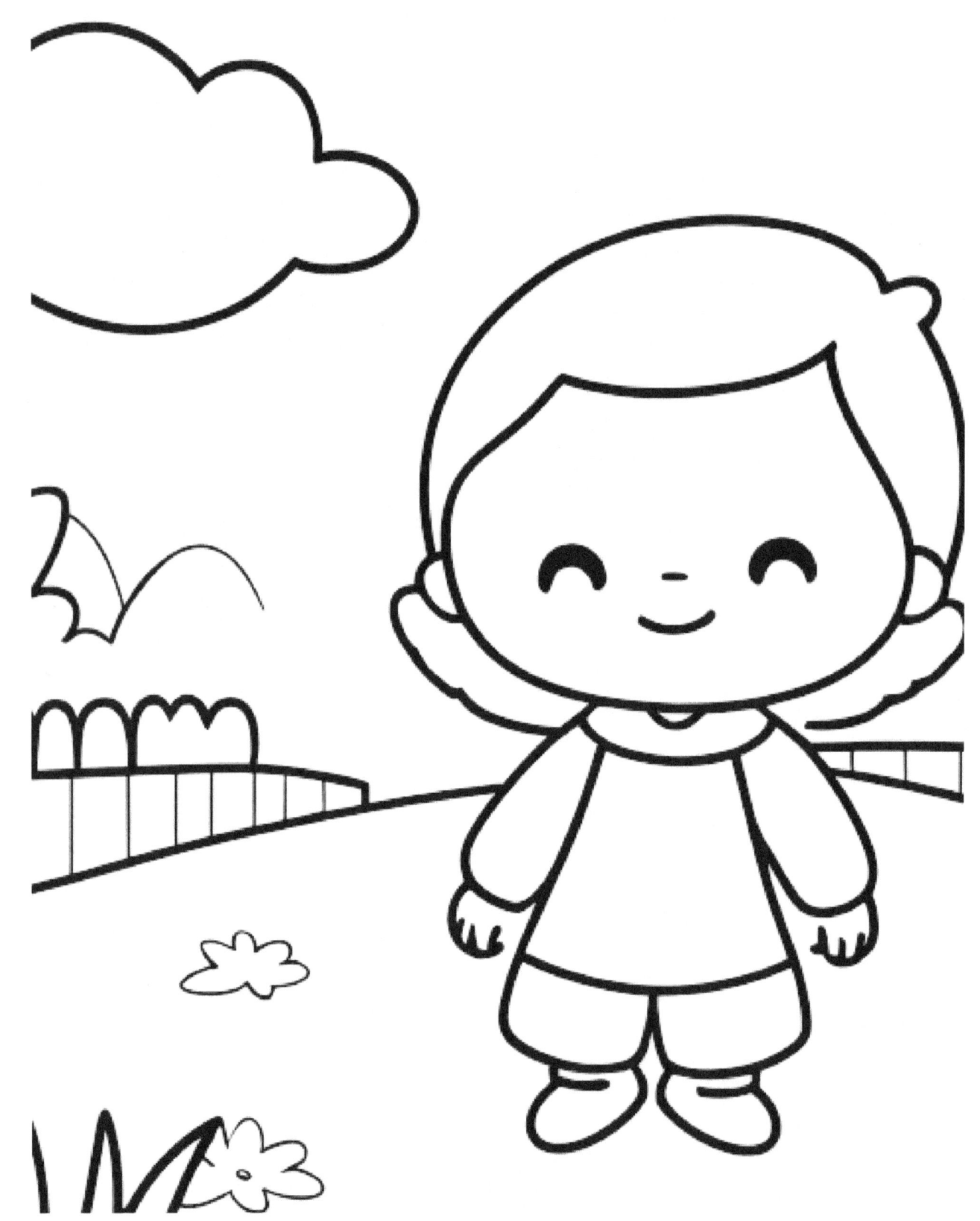

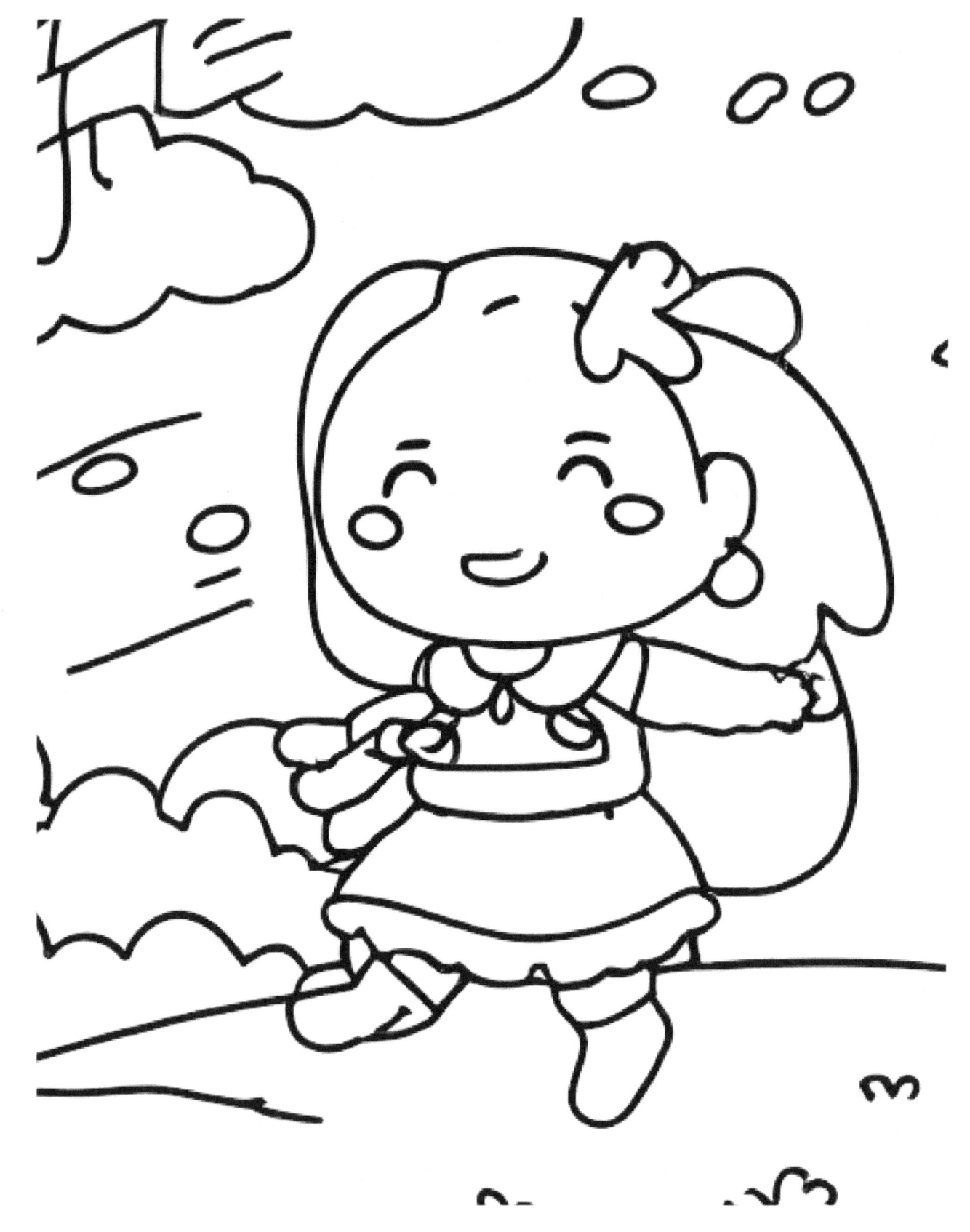

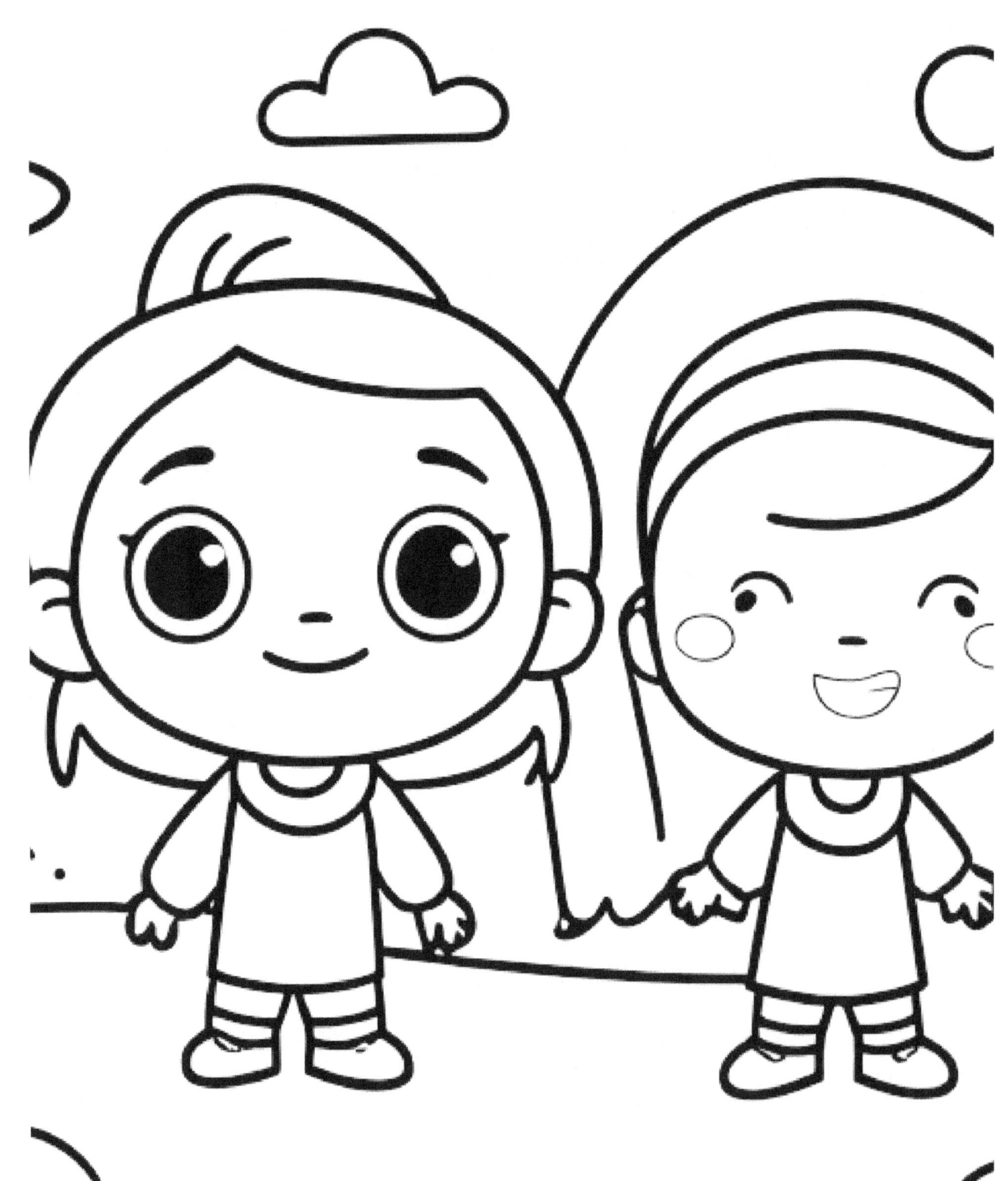

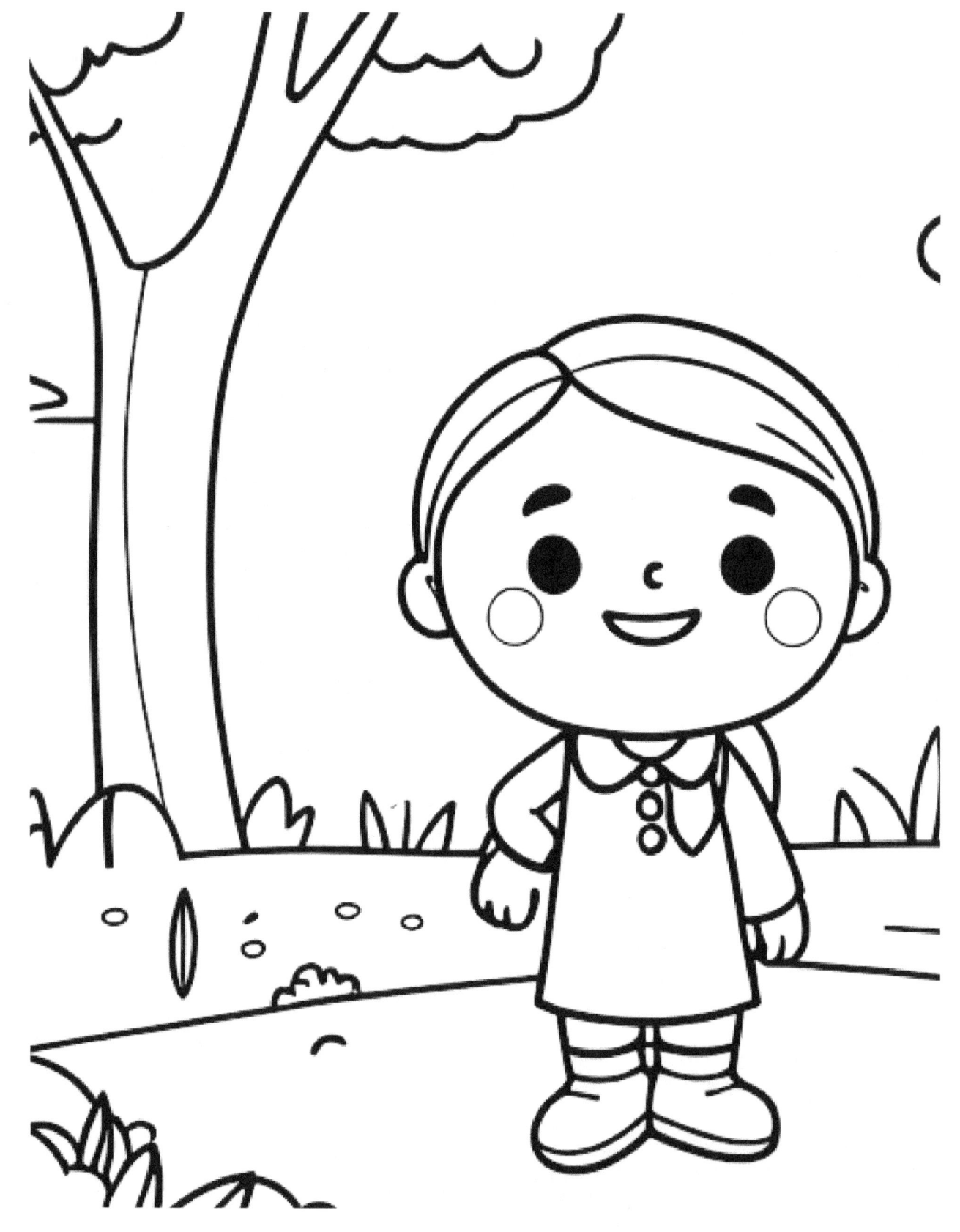

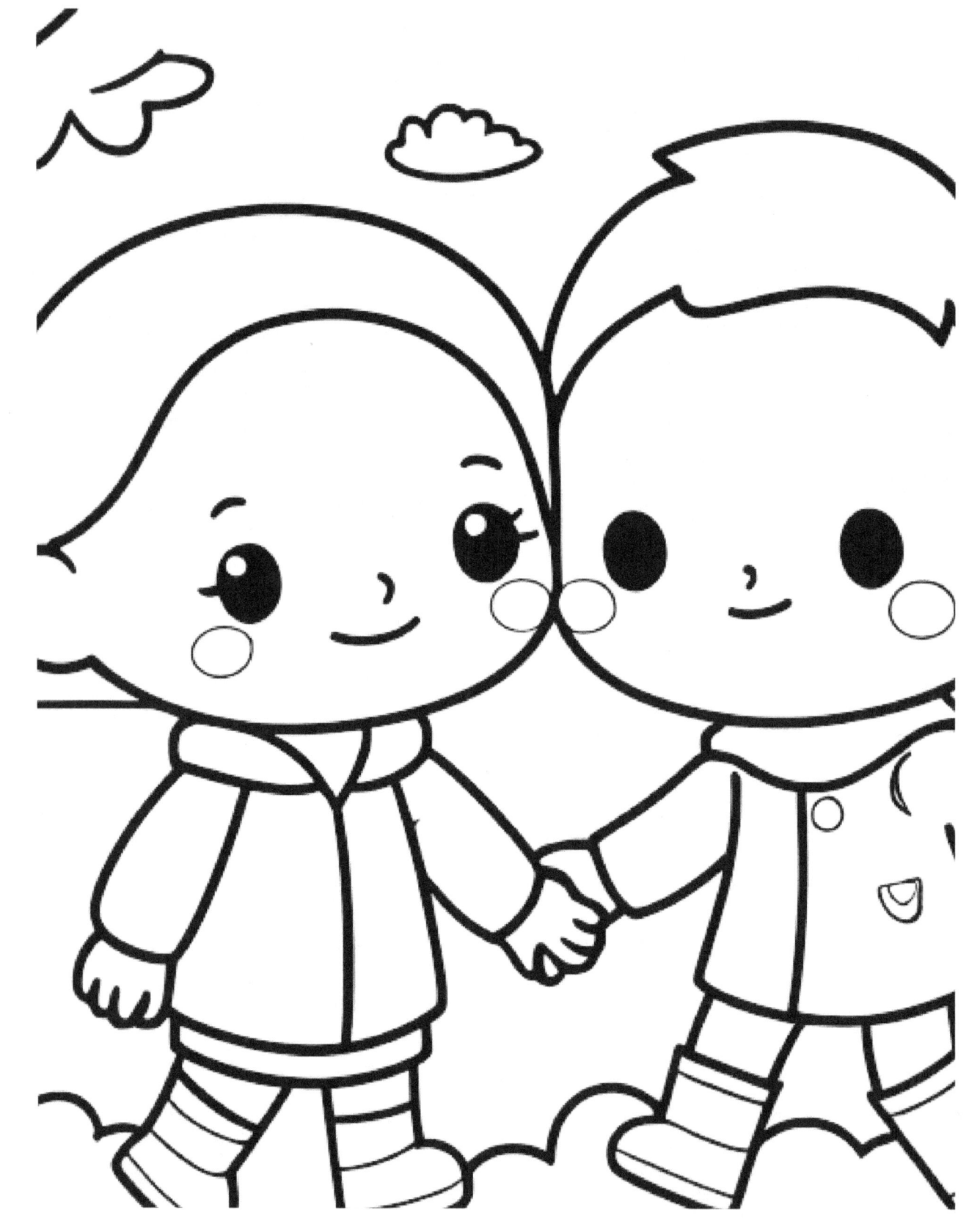

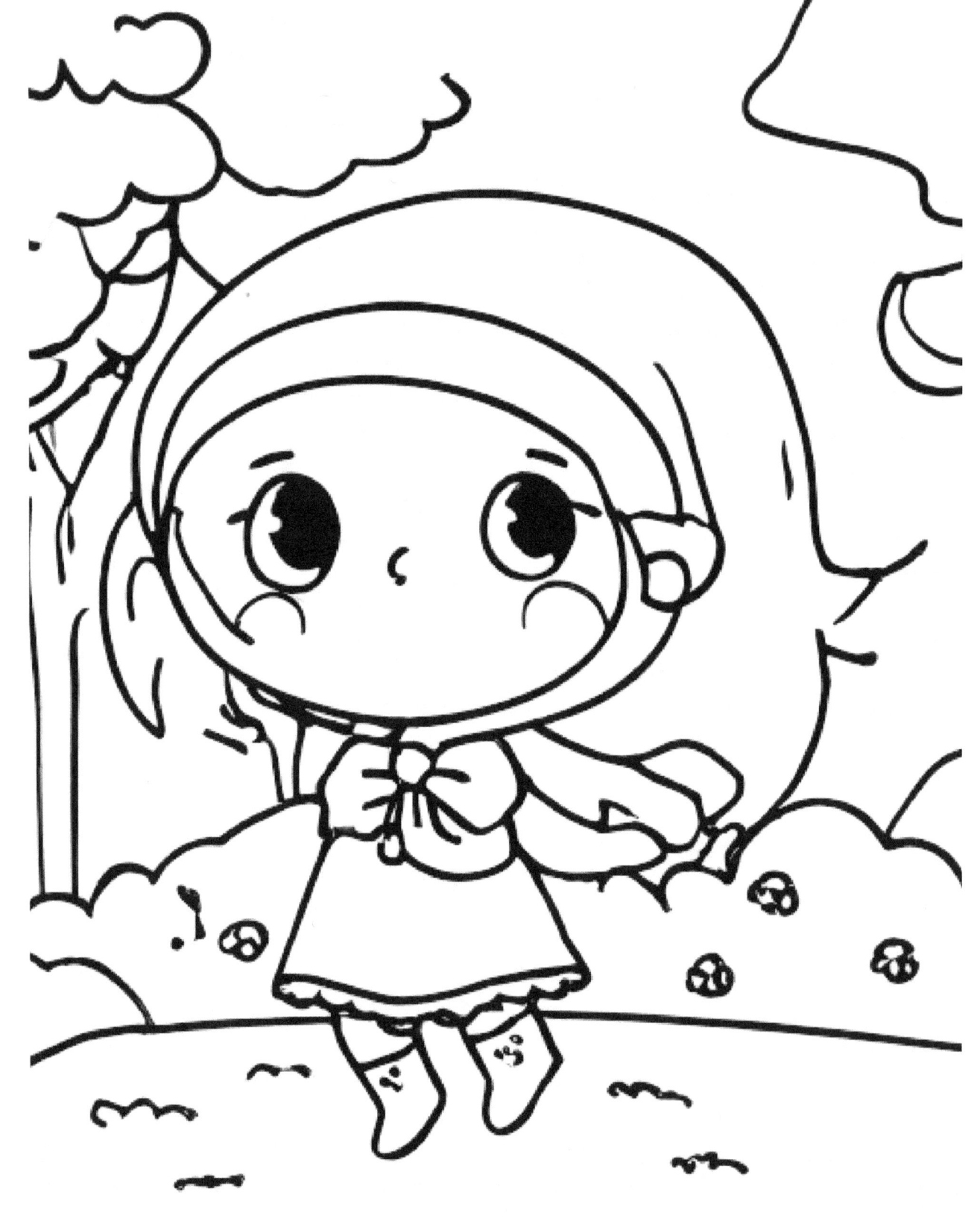

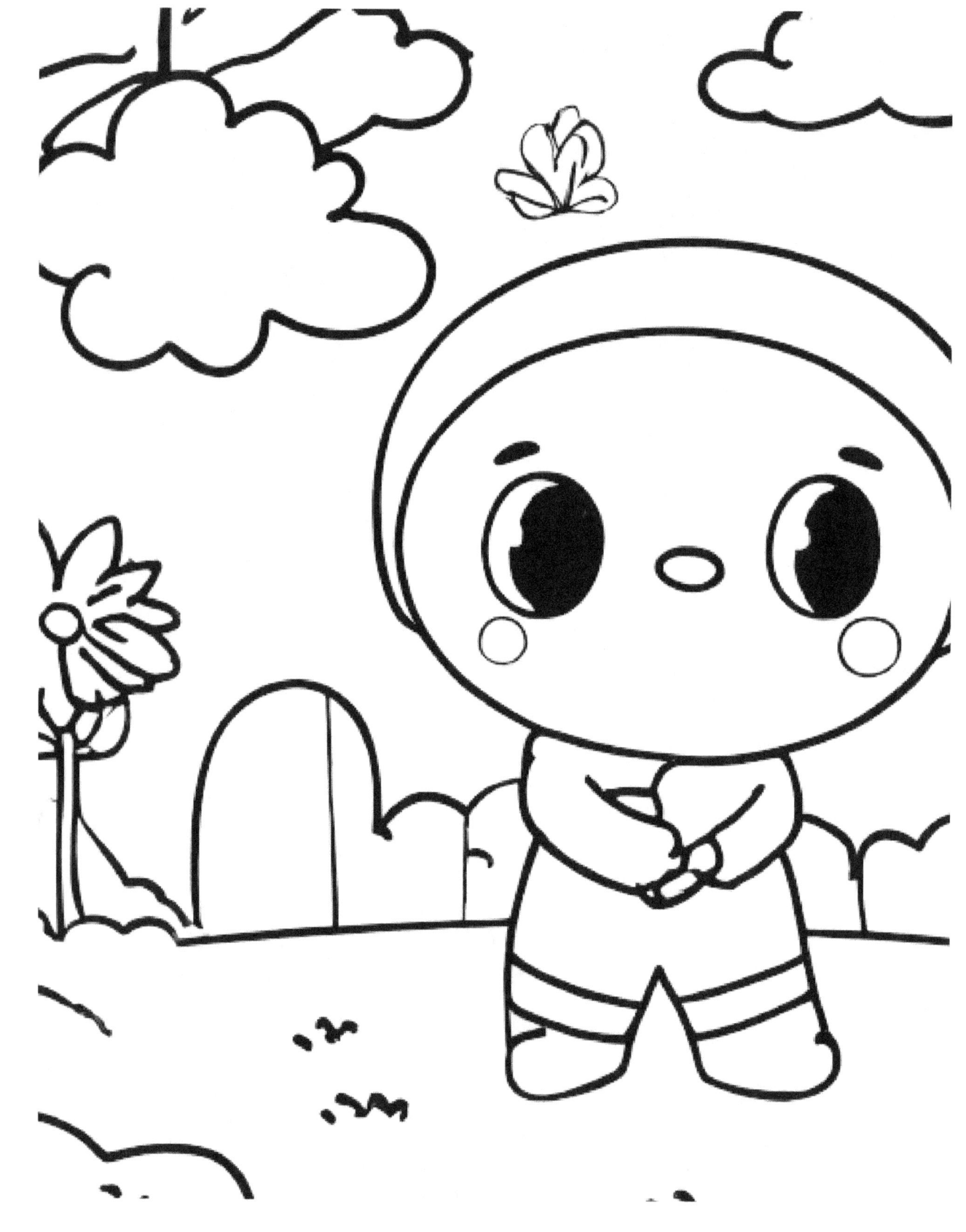

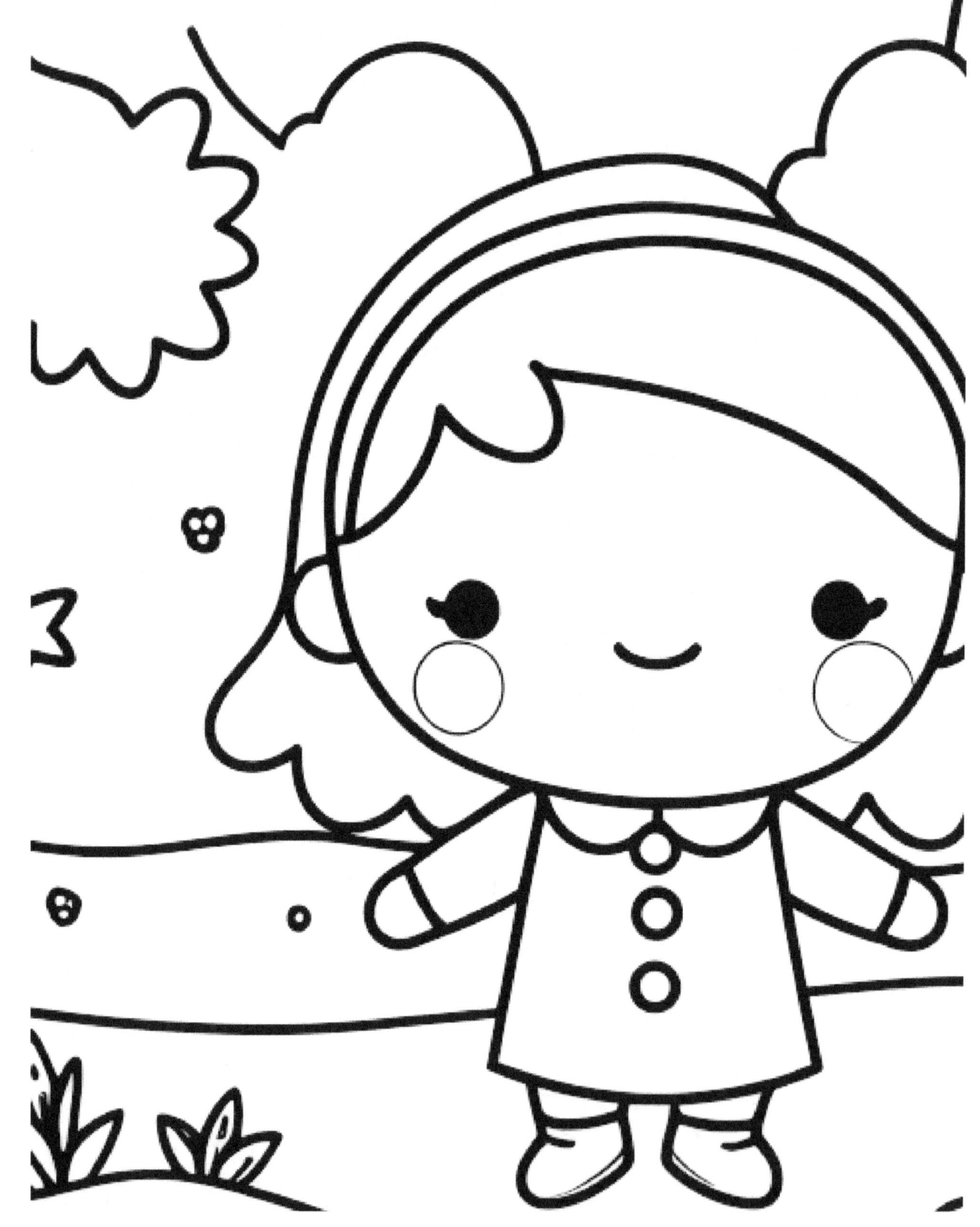